RUBANK Treasures for TUBA

ONLINE MEDIA INCLUDED
Audio Recordings
Printable Piano Accompaniments

PLAYBACK+
Speed • Pitch • Balance • Loop

T0065890

CONTENTS

To access recordings and PDF piano accompaniments, go to:
www.halleonard.com/mylibrary

Enter Code
4296-3164-5819-0746

ISBN 978-1-4950-7510-0

HAL•LEONARD®
7777 W. BLUEMOUND RD. P.O. BOX 13819 MILWAUKEE, WI 53213

Visit Hal Leonard Online at
www.halleonard.com

In the Hall of the Mountain King

from *Peer Gynt Suite No. 1, Op. 46*

Tuba

Edvard Grieg
Arranged by G.E. Holmes

00196892

The Leprechauns' Patrol

Tuba

Harold L. Walters

5

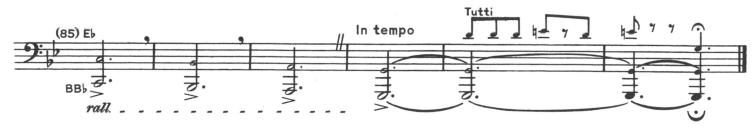

5

Andante and Allegro

Tuba

Robert Clérisse
Transcribed by H. Voxman

Toreador's Song
from *Carmen*

Tuba

Georges Bizet
Arranged by G.E. Holmes

8

The Mariner

Tito Mattei
Arranged by Harold L. Walters

Tuba

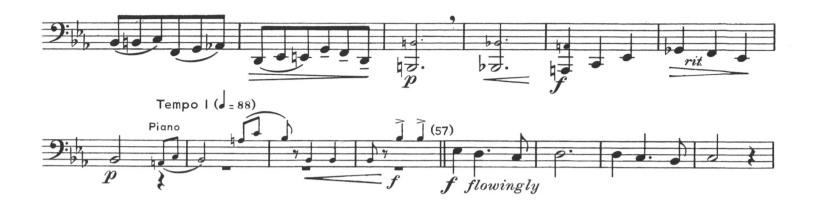

Blow the Man Down
Sea Shanty with Variations

Tuba

Harold L. Walters

00196892

molto rit.

Meno mosso (♩ = 68)

(67)   (75)

cantabile

rit

Con fuoco

ff   Piano   ad lib.   accel.   3   3   𝆏 rall.   dolce

Allegro con moto (♩. = 112 or faster)

Piano   (87)   (95)

𝆏   f   p   mp

f   p

(103)

f   p

2   (112)

f   ff

Hero of the Brass

Tuba

George E. Worth

Allegro

accel.

*This page
intentionally
blank*

Andante Cantabile
from Concerto for Trombone

Tuba

Nicolai Rimsky-Korsakov
Transcribed by H. Voxman

00196892

Behehemoth

Tuba

Hale A. VanderCook

00196892

TRIO

Moderato pomposo

17

00196892

Adagio and Finale
from Concertino for Trombone

Tuba

Charles Gaucet
Transcribed by H. Voxman

FINALE

Allegro moderato

Emmett's Lullaby
Theme and Variations
as performed by William Bell

Tuba

Joseph K. Emmett
Transcribed by G.E. Holmes

00196892

* Designates a recording "click"
(accomp. recording only)

Concertpiece

Tuba

H. Painparé
Revised by H. Voxman

* Designates a recording "click" (accomp. recording only)

24